PAULIST BIBLE STUDY PROGRAM

Galatians and Romans

WORKBOOK

Workbook by Patricia Datchuck Sánchez
Video Scripts by Elliott Maloney, O.S.B.
Prayers by Rea McDonnell, S.S.N.D.

PAULIST PRESS

New York/Mahwah

Acknowledgments

Cover photo, *Conversion of St. Paul*, courtesy of Alinari/Art Resource, NY.

Faith Sharing Principles are reprinted from RENEW, copyright © 1987 by the Roman Catholic Archdiocese of Newark, New Jersey. Used by permission.

ISBN: 0-8091-9416-3

Published by Paulist Press
997 Macarthur Boulevard
Mahwah, New Jersey 07430

Printed and bound in the United States of America

Dear Friends,

It is a pleasure to present to you our Paulist Bible Study Program. The Paulist Bible Study Program is designed to help adults understand the Bible in the light of contemporary biblical scholarship and to use the Bible as a source of prayer, reflection, and action. It relates the study of the Bible to the liturgy, to the Church, and to our daily lives. Those who long to know more about the Bible, based on the authentic Catholic tradition and the most responsible and best biblical scholarship, have a rich experience awaiting them.

Kevin A. Lynch, C.S.P.
Publisher

INTRODUCTION

Welcome to the Paulist Bible Study Program and to this third unit on the New Testament.

In this unit you will focus on the themes and message of St. Paul's letters to the Galatians and Romans. This Workbook will serve as a reading guide to the Bible and to your companion text, *Pillars of Paul's Gospel*, by John F. O'Grady. Each week it will point out what passages of the Bible you should read and what parts of the companion text are focused on these passages.

The Bible in the Life of the Church

The emergence of popular interest in the Bible among Catholics stems from the Second Vatican Council. Along with the new emphasis on the Scriptures during the Eucharist and other sacramental celebrations, the Council called upon all members of the Church to grow in their knowledge and love of the Bible:

> Just as the life of the Church grows through persistent participation in the Eucharistic mystery, so we may hope for a new surge of spiritual vitality from intensified veneration for God's Word (*Dogmatic Constitution on Divine Revelation*, 26).

The vision of the central place of the Scriptures which the Council set forth is becoming more and more a reality.

> The Church has always venerated the divine Scriptures just as she venerates the body of the Lord, since from the table of both the Word of God and of the body of

Christ she unceasingly receives and offers to the faithful the bread of life, especially in the sacred liturgy. She has always regarded the Scriptures together with sacred tradition as the supreme rule of faith, and will ever do so (*Dogmatic Constitution on Divine Revelation*, 21).

Our hope is that this program will be yet another resource which will take the process of integrating Scripture into the life of the Church one step further.

Jesus' Own Bible Study Model

In 1986, Archbishop Roger Mahony of Los Angeles issued a pastoral letter entitled "The Bible in the Life of the Church." One part of the letter reflects on Jesus' own approach to teaching the Scriptures to his disciples as he walked with two of them on the road to Emmaus (Lk 24:13-35). Archbishop Mahony's reflections on this passage are a fitting introduction to our study of the Bible.

> The two disciples are on their way from Jerusalem to Emmaus when Jesus—his appearance hidden—joins them. He responds to their bewilderment by "interpreting for them every passage of Scripture which referred to him." This was the most clear example of Jesus sharing the Scriptures that we find in the gospels. For our own Bible study to be beneficial, then, we too must open our hearts and lives to allow Jesus to unlock the meaning of his message for us.

> But two additional elements in the Emmaus journey are also required to validate our own experience of the Scriptures. First, our Scripture study must lead toward, center around, and flow from the Eucharist—the Mass. It was only in "the breaking of the bread" that the full meaning of Jesus' explanations became clear to the two men journeying to Emmaus. As Catholics, we too must always focus our Bible studies in and through the Eucharist. And secondly, we must be guided in our Scripture studies through "Simon Peter—the Church." Recall that the two men returned in haste to Jerusalem where they were greeted with: "The Lord has been raised! It is true! He has appeared to Simon." This validation by Peter—by the Church—is essential to our authentic understanding of the Word of God.

The Importance of Commitment

What are your goals for your participation in this program? As you begin, take a few moments to reflect upon your goals and jot them down. These may involve gaining some knowledge, but don't omit other possible gains such as growing in your spirituality or prayer life or building community within your parish. Any goal worth achieving requires commitment. During this program you are invited to make a commitment to grow in your understanding and appreciation of the Bible. All commitments require the most precious of commodities: time. In this case, you are committing yourself to be present at the eight sessions and to participate in the learning process.

What follows is a description of the various steps you should take to prepare for and to follow up on a meeting. Only you can determine how much time you have to spend on these steps. Not everything needs to be done now. Hopefully, the Paulist Bible Study Program will provide you with the resources to continue your own study well after a particular unit ends.

In addition to a time commitment, you are making a commitment to the other participants in your group. You bring unique gifts and experience to this study of the Bible that will enrich your co-learners. The steps below offer some tips on how you can both share your own insights and enable others to share theirs.

Preparing for the Meeting

Each week you will be meeting with others to reflect on the Scriptures and the parts of the companion text. Before you engage in the activities in this book, follow the steps outlined for each session in the section called Preparation.

1. Prayerfully read the appointed Bible passages.

2. Read the assigned portion of the companion text. You may want to read a little bit each day to coordinate with your prayerful reading of the Bible. Many find it helpful to mark the text for key parts or to jot down questions that may arise during a reading.

3. Read the Focus and Review of Contents before the meeting. If you have time, try to work on responses to the review questions. Your companion text also has review questions after each chapter which will be helpful.

During the Meeting

Each session is designed to last two hours. You may find that the suggested times for each element vary for your group. Encourage the sharing and interaction within your group rather than feeling bound by time. Here are the steps for each session and some suggestions on how to make use of them.

Opening Prayer (5 minutes)
Place yourself and your group in God's presence, asking for the guidance of the Holy Spirit during the upcoming session.

Review of Contents (25 minutes)
This section gives you the opportunity to express what you have learned and to learn from the insights of others. If you have questions other than those raised in the review,

bring them up at this time. While your Program Leader cannot be expected to have all the answers, he or she may be able to help you find the answers to your questions.

Video (20 minutes)

The video is designed to enrich your learning by providing the visual dimension of what you are studying. Before viewing the program, look at the highlight questions. Jot down the answers as you watch the program. Afterward, there is a brief time for you to raise questions or make a comment.

Learning Activity (25 minutes)

During this segment, you will work with others in an activity to further integrate the meaning of the Scripture you have read and to apply it to your life.

Faith Sharing (25 minutes)

The following suggestions, borrowed from RENEW, are helpful guidelines for faith sharing:

- The entire faith-sharing process is seen as prayer, i.e., listening to the Word of God as broken by others' experience.
- Constant attention to respect, honesty, and openness for each person will assist the group's growth.
- Each person shares on the level where he or she feels comfortable.
- Silence is a vital part of the total process of faith sharing. Participants are given time to reflect before any sharing begins, and a period of comfortable silence might occur between individual sharings.
- Persons are encouraged to wait to share a second time until others who wish to do so have contributed.
- The entire group is responsible for participating and faith sharing.
- Confidentiality is essential, allowing each person to share honestly.
- Reaching beyond the group in action and response is essential for the growth of individuals, the group, and the Church.

Closing Prayer (10 minutes)

Having shared our faith together, we conclude with prayer. Join in the spirit of the prayer service by singing, praying, and listening to the Word of God.

After the Meeting

Journaling

For each session, at least one journal idea is suggested. You may wish to keep a journal either to do these activities, or simply to write your own reflections.

Additional Resources

Each week a number of sources are referred to for further reading and study. Your parish may have purchased these books for a parish resource library or you may obtain them from Paulist Press. Your Program Leader has further information. You may wish to consult these sources for continued study after the unit ends.

1. Paul, the Man, His Mission, His Message

FOCUS

More than any other New Testament author, Paul enables those who read his writings to meet him "up close and personal." In fact, he affords us no other option. To read Paul's letters is to meet the man, to share in his struggles, to experience his vision, to burn with his sense of purpose and mission. To meet Paul is to meet Christ and to be confronted with the power of the gospel.

Any attempt to read Paul passively is futile. He will provoke us with his passion; he will draw us to experience, as he did, the transforming quality of encountering Christ. Paul's commitment to Jesus stirs us to rethink our own commitment; his faith urges us to rekindle our own.

Paul's pioneering insights into the good news of salvation challenged his contemporaries to expand their provincial and limited perception of God's gifts unto absolute and universal proportions. With untiring constancy Paul aided his contemporaries in implementing the gospel challenge with the varied pastoral needs and ever-changing complexion of the growing Church. His efforts at translating the good news into lived faith continue to engage the attention and energies of all who believe in Jesus.

During this initial session, we will meet Paul, "up close and personal" and share with him and with one another both the blessings and the sufferings which are inherent to the Christian life.

OPENING PRAYER

Invitation to Prayer

Leader:
Paul writes to the community in Galatia that God had called and chosen Paul even before he was born. To celebrate God's choice of Paul and God's call to us, we will open with a prayer-dialogue based on the Servant Songs of Isaiah.

Reader:
God formed me in the womb to be God's own servant, saying: "I will make you a light to the nations, that my salvation may reach to the ends of the earth" (cf. Is 49:5–6).

All pray:
We adore you, O Christ, and we praise you, because you are God's servant, God's light, God's salvation for us.

Reader:
God has given me the tongue of a teacher and skill to console the weary. God has sharpened my hearing. How lovely on the mountains are the feet of those who bring good news! (cf. Is 50:4; 52:7).

All pray:
We praise and thank you, risen Lord, that you shared your gospel and your mission with Paul.

Reader:

Your light will break forth like the dawn. Your wound will be healed. Your light will rise like dawn out of darkness. You will be like a well watered garden, like a spring whose waters never fail (cf. Is 58:8, 10, 11).

All pray:

Help us, through our study of Scripture, to meet and know you ever more deeply, risen Christ. Let your Word be our light and a spring of energy deep within us. Transform our hearts through the power of your Word so that we, like Paul and with Paul, may carry your light and your energy to our world. Amen.

GETTING STARTED

1. What is your ethnic background? How has your particular ethnic background enriched and/or influenced your family and/or social life? Your political views? Your faith life?

2. Paul was the multi-talented heir of a mixed ethnic background. Born in Tarsus, the busy capital city of the Roman Empire's province of Cilicia, Paul was a Jew, well educated in the religious traditions and literature of his people. He was fluent in Greek language and thought—an influence stemming from the time of Alexander the Great in the fourth century B.C., when Greek culture, art, and philosophy permeated the ancient Near Eastern world.

In what ways did the variety of ethnic elements in Paul's background influence him and his ministry?

3. Like Jesus, Paul lived during the period of peace enforced by Rome (*Pax Romana*). To maintain that peace and to promote unity and trade among all its occupied lands, Rome built a vast system of over 250,000 miles of paved roads, many of which are still in use today. Look at the map of the Roman Empire in the first century in the companion text (p. 13) and at the list of Paul's letters and the locations from which they were written (p. 15). In what way did Roman engineering aid Paul in his ministry?

4. Paul's letters were among the earliest writings of the New Testament and comprise approximately one quarter of it. Yet in all his letters, Paul never recounted a healing, a parable, or even a saying of Jesus. Nevertheless Paul claimed to preach the gospel of Christ (Gal 1:11–12).

In your companion text, read the summary of the gospel Paul preached (p. 45).

a. From what you know about Paul, describe his missionary method for spreading the gospel.

b. Why do you think Paul used the literary form of a *letter* in his gospel ministry?

c. Do Paul's first-century letters have any relevance for believers on the brink of the twenty-first century? Explain.

VIDEO

Paul the Pharisee Becomes Zealous for Christ

As you view the video, please make note of the following:

1. Why was Tarsus considered to be a rather sophisticated Hellenistic town?

Center of commerce & art

2. What led Paul to persecute the early Christians?

info from Jewish. He was a pharisee.

3. List two or three characteristics of Paul that made him an exceptional apostle of Christ.

fervor, intelligence

BREAK
(10 minutes)

LEARNING ACTIVITY

1. Paul's great work for Christ and for the Church was rooted in his experience of the risen Jesus on the way to Damascus. Both Paul, in his letters, and Luke, in the Acts of the Apostles, have provided us with several descriptions of that profound encounter. Admittedly, finite human words and human symbols are, at best, limited tools with which to describe infinite realities; nevertheless, Luke's graphic portrayal of Paul's experience invites us to approach and to appreciate the wondrous nature of that event.

In your small groups, read aloud one of the accounts of Paul's religious experience according to Luke: Acts 9:1–19, Acts 22:3–16, or Acts 26:2–18.

a. Why is it significant that Paul is on a journey?

b. Light is a featured element in Paul's experience of Jesus. What do you think the light signified?

c. Each of Luke's accounts includes the same exchange between the risen Lord and Paul: "Saul, Saul, why are you persecuting me?" He (Paul) said, "Who are you, sir?" The reply came, "I am Jesus whom you are persecuting."

What are the implications of this exchange?

2. Paul, in his writings, cited his initial encounter with Jesus as the source of his apostolic identity and mandate. He described that profound event in terms of the changes that took effect in his life. Paul would spend the rest of his life attempting to name this experience for himself and

calling others to recognize and to name similar experiences for themselves.

a. Read Galatians 1:11–24 and 1 Corinthians 15:8–11. How did Paul account for the changes that took place in his life? Was his transformation something he initiated? What was his role in it?

b. Paul described his encounter with the risen Lord in terms of revelation and a call from God.

Today, we call an experience like Paul's a conversion or *metanoia*. *Metanoia* is a Greek term which means a radical change of heart, mind, and orientation. From what you know about Paul, identify the changes that took place in his life and ministry.

3. Through the Scriptures, we can share in the religious experiences of our heroes and heroines in the faith. Choose one of the following texts and read it aloud in your small group:

Ruth 1:16–18
1 Samuel 3:1–11
Isaiah 6:1–8
Jeremiah 1:4–10
Amos 7:14–15
Luke 19:1–9
John 4:4–29, 39–42

How does the experience of the person in the passage you read compare to that of Paul? What are the similarities? What are the differences?

FAITH SHARING

In the first Christian century, believers in Jesus identified themselves as followers of the Way (Acts 18:25) and described the life of faith as a journey (1 Pt 1:17). In the fifth century, St. Augustine called the Church "a pilgrim in a foreign land, pressing forward amid the persecutions of the world and the consolations of God" (*City of God*). In the twentieth century, the participants at the Second Vatican Council affirmed the nature of the Church as a pilgrim people, journeying toward the Father (*Dogmatic Constitution on the Church*, 7).

Like Paul on the road to Damascus, each of us is on a journey. Like Paul, each of us has religious experiences which affect the course and orientation of our journey through life. Paul's experience was dramatic; thereafter everything he did and said was affected by and rooted in that experience.

1. How would you describe your personal religious experience(s)?

2. What effect have your religious experiences had upon your particular journey through life?

3. Have others helped you in understanding and/or responding to your religious experiences?

CLOSING PRAYER

A Call to Remember

Reading (2 Cor 4:3–10)

All:
Thanks be to God.

A Call to Respond

All pray:
With you is the fountain of life
And in your light we are bathed in light.

All pray:
. . . in Christ's light, you are bathed in light.

All:
Our Father and Mother, who art in heaven . . .
For the kingdon, etc.

Concluding Song

"Earthen Vessels" by John Foley, S.J.

FOLLOW-UP

A. Journaling

Paul's decision for Christ and his service to the gospel brought both blessings and sufferings into his life. Reflect on your own decision for Christ and the gospel. What blessings and sufferings has your commitment brought into your life? What effect have these had upon your commitment?

B. Additional Resources

1. Read John F. O'Grady, *Pillars of Paul's Gospel: Galatians and Romans*, Chapters 1, 2, and 4.

2. Read *The Catholic Study Bible*, "Paul and His Writings," RG 470–472.

3. Read Joseph Plevnick, S.J., *What Are They Saying About Paul?*, Chapter 1, pp. 5–27.

2. New Wine, New Wineskins!

Preparation

- Read Galatians 1–2.
- Read Acts 16:6, 18:23.
- Read *Pillars of Paul's Gospel: Galatians and Romans*, Chapters 3, 5, and 6.
- Reflect on the FOCUS statement and REVIEW OF CONTENTS questions.

FOCUS

As a result of his encounter with the risen Lord on the Damascus road, Paul was a changed man. Changed forever was his understanding of himself and his purpose in life. Changed forever was his attitude toward the law and toward the justification attributed to the law. Changed was his relationship toward Gentiles and toward sinners.

As a Jew who had come to believe in the all-sufficient and universal power of Jesus' saving death, Paul had also come to realize that the old wineskin of Judaism was incapable of receiving the new wine of the gospel. Thereafter he wholeheartedly and relentlessly applied himself to a dual task: (1) Paul preached to the Gentiles the good news of salvation, free and unencumbered by the law and the influence of Jewish tradition; and (2) he fearlessly defended his right to do so and confronted all who sought to alter or in any way hamper the gospel he preached.

In this session we will experience the strength of Paul's conviction and his dauntless courage in the face of adversity. Through his letter to the believers in Galatia, we shall gain an indirect knowledge of his opponents and of the threat they posed to his apostolic authority and service.

To many of his contemporaries, Paul appeared to be a "loose cannon" and a deterrent to the development of the Church. But as we become more aware of the radical and revolutionary quality of Paul's insights, we shall also become more aware that his vision of God and of salvation was precisely the vision of the loving and merciful Father which Jesus had come to impart.

OPENING PRAYER

Opening Song

"Sing a New Song" by Dan Schutte, S.J.

Call to Praise (Pss 27 and 34, selected verses, adapted)

Leader:
I bring you God's GOOD news! You are loved! Unconditionally. Faithfully.

Right side:
God alone is my light and my salvation. Whom should I fear?

Left side:
One thing I ask, this I want: to live with my God all the days of my life.

Right side:
I want to gaze on God's beauty, and to look for God everywhere.

Left side:
Come, my heart cries out, come and seek God's face. The Lord only is my salvation.

Right side:
Look to God. Then our faces will not blush with shame. Our faces are radiant with joy.

Left side:
Come, friends, and I will teach you the good news of God's abundant and faithful kindness.

All:
Glory to God who loves us.
Glory to Jesus who saves us.
Glory to the Spirit who sends us to proclaim this good news.
Amen. Amen.

REVIEW OF CONTENTS

1. Paul's encounter with the risen Lord transformed his life. When he handed on the good news he had received, Paul challenged others to be similarly transformed.

With the help of your companion text, identify the changes made by the Galatians as a result of Paul's preaching of the gospel. See companion text (pp. 49, 51).

2. After Paul left the Galatian churches and moved on to other missions, those who opposed his authority and his message demanded that the Galatians make other changes in their lives.

a. Who were Paul's opponents?

b. What were the changes they required of the Galatians?

3. When news reached Paul of the situation in Galatia, he reacted rapidly and vehemently.

a. How did Paul defend his service of the gospel?

b. From whom did Paul claim to derive his authority to preach?

4. Paul accused Kephas (Peter) and other Jews of hypocrisy (Gal 2:11–14). The word hypocrite is derived from a Greek term which originally referred to an actor in a play. The companion text lists additional meanings for the word hypocrite (cf. p. 58). Given this background, do you think Paul was correct in his assessment of Peter? Why?

VIDEO

The Background of the Letter to the Galatians

As you view the video, please make note of the following:

1. What circumstance led to the love and affection Paul had for the Galatians?

_____

_____

2. Why did Paul take exception to the Galatians' confusion over the Judaizers?

_____

_____

3. What prompted the confrontation between Paul and Peter? How was the matter resolved?

_____

_____

BREAK
(10 minutes)

LEARNING ACTIVITY

1. Because of the seemingly revolutionary quality of his insight, some modern critics have argued that "Paul invented Christianity." Even his contemporaries questioned the authenticity of his ideas. Imagine that you are a Jewish Christian elder serving on the council of elders in Jerusalem. Paul has traveled to Jerusalem to present the gospel he has been preaching to the Gentiles. As an eyewitness to Jesus' ministry, you have been asked to hear him and to evaluate his message. Citing his own life as an example, Paul explains that although he had excelled in righteousness and in the observance of the law, it had not resulted in his justification. Simply put, Paul explains that justification means "being right with God." Through revelation, Paul claims to have learned of the power of Jesus' saving death and of the free gift of God's grace for sinners. Therefore he preaches the good news that justification or "being right with God" comes not through the law, but through faith in Jesus Christ.

Read Matthew 9:11–13, Mark 2:22, Luke 18:9–14, John 3:16–17.

a. How does Paul's gospel as summarized in Galatians 2:15–21 compare to the teachings of Jesus?

b. As a Christian elder of Jewish origin, you are familiar with the Book of Isaiah and the description of the suffering servant which reads, "Through his suffering, my servant shall justify many, and their guilt he shall bear" (Is 53:11).

Where in Galatians 1–2 does Paul indicate that he understood Jesus' death in similar terms?

c. As an elder of the Church, would you approve or censor Paul's gospel? Would you offer him any advice?

2. When Paul preached in Galatia, many who heard him responded enthusiastically and accepted the gospel in full faith. But, when others came after Paul, preaching a gospel dependent on the works of the law (Mosaic law, circumcision), the Galatians were swayed to accept their teachings.

How can you account for the Galatians' ready acceptance of this later "gospel"?

3. Some Catholics, upset by the changes set in motion by the Second Vatican Council, experienced a situation similar to that of the believers in Galatia. In an attempt to renew itself in its faith and commitment in service to Jesus Christ, the post-Vatican II Church placed less emphasis on prescribed rules, penances, and obligations and more emphasis on personal freedom, responsible choices, and conscience. Many were heard to complain, "We don't know what we're supposed to do anymore."

Pretend that you are Paul. Using Galatians 2, compose a few words of advice for twentieth-century believers who are upset with the new emphasis on freedom and personal responsibility brought about by the Council decrees.

FAITH SHARING

Before the Damascus encounter, Paul understood his religious commitment in terms of his zealous conformity to the law. After his experience on the Damascus road, Paul understood his religious commitment as faithful adherence to the person of Jesus Christ, crucified and risen. He expressed his realization in these words: "Yet I live, no longer I, but Christ lives in me; insofar as I now live in the flesh, I live by faith in the Son of God who has loved me and given himself up for me" (Gal 2:20).

Before the Damascus event, the guiding principle in Paul's life was an external one; after his Damascus experience, the guiding principle for Paul's life became both interior and personal.

1. How did this realization affect the way Paul lived his life?

2. Through our baptism, we are incorporated into Christ's death and resurrection. With Paul we can proclaim, "Christ lives in me." What does it mean to you, "to be crucified with Christ"? What does it mean to you, "to live by faith in the Son of God"?

3. Have you or has someone close to you had an external reality as the guiding principle of life? Share the effects of that guiding principle.

4. Have you or has someone close to you had a guiding principle that has been interior or personal? Share the effects of that guiding principle.

CLOSING PRAYER

A Call to Remember

Reading (Gal 2:15–16)

All respond:
"Yet I live, no longer I, but Christ lives in me" (Gal 2:20).

Sharing the Good News

All:
Our Father and Mother, who art in heaven . . .
For the kingdom, etc.

Concluding Song

"Sing a New Song" (chorus only)
or
"Song of Good News" by Willard Jabusch

REMINDER FOR NEXT TIME:
For the next session, each participant should bring a photograph of himself or herself as a child (not as an infant, however) which will be used during the Closing Prayer.

FOLLOW-UP

A. Journaling

Reread Galatians 1–2.

Because of the power of the gospel which had transformed his life, Paul became a fearless and sometimes fierce defender of the faith. He did not shrink from conflict. So strong were his convictions that he confronted the Galatians, his opponents, and even Peter.

Reflect upon the transforming power of the gospel in your own life. Have you experienced a similar strength and conviction? How do you deal with conflict and/or confrontation?

B. Additional Resource

1. Read *The Catholic Study Bible*, "Galatians," RG 505–507 and the introduction to Galatians, pp. 293–294 of the New Testament.

3. A New People of God

Preparation

- Read Galatians 3–4.
- Read *Pillars of Paul's Gospel: Galatians and Romans,* Chapter 7.
- Reflect on the FOCUS statement and REVIEW OF CONTENTS questions.

FOCUS

As one who had begun "to live by faith in the Son of God," Paul had come to understand that the parameters of salvation had been redefined by Jesus' death on the cross. No longer were the law and circumcision necessary requisites; no longer could membership in the people of God be defined in terms of ethnicity or human achievement. Paul had learned that justification does not depend on *what we do* or on *who we are* but on *who we have become* in Christ Jesus.

Because of the saving death of Jesus, the people of God would ever after be defined in terms of grace and faith. Because of Jesus, all who had been enslaved by legalism and by sin would be gifted with the Spirit and thereby freed to become children of the Father and heirs of God's promises.

During this session, as we continue to study Paul's gospel, we shall experience his irritation with the Galatians who had digressed from the good news as he had preached it among them. Drawing on the Galatians' own experience, on history, and on Scrip-

---

ture, Paul makes a powerful case for the priority of faith over the law.

As he challenges the Galatians to remember and to realize their dignity as the free and faithful people of God, Paul issues a similar challenge to us. With Paul's help we shall remember who we are, and recommit ourselves in faith to all we have become and all that is ours in Christ Jesus.

OPENING PRAYER

Invitation to Prayer

Leader:
Good news! We are God's own, not because of what we do, but because of God's grace and our faith in Jesus' saving love.

Let us respond to this good news, this gospel of Paul, by praying an adaptation of Psalm 103 together.

All:
Bless the Lord, all my being, as I surrender myself to God.

Reader:
God pardons all our iniquities and heals all our pain, saving our life from destruction, crowning us with God's own kindness and compassion.

All:
Bless the Lord, all my being, as I surrender myself to God.

Reader:
Merciful and gracious is our God, slow to anger and

abounding in kindness. God does not deal with us according to our sins, for God remembers how small we are.

All:
Bless the Lord, all my being, as I surrender myself to God.

Reader:
As far as the east is from the west, so far has God put our faults from us. As a father has compassion on his children, as a mother cares for the child of her womb, so our God is tender with us. God knows how we are formed. God remembers that we are dust.

All:
Bless the Lord, all my being, as I surrender myself to God.

Reader:
Our days are like grass. Like flowers of the field we bloom. Then the wind sweeps over us and we are gone. But the kindness of God to us lasts forever, God's faithfulness to the end of time.

All:
Bless the Lord, all my being, as I surrender myself to God.

Leader:
Let us sit in silence for a few moments and let our images of God rise to consciousness. Who is this God to whom we say we surrender? And how do we feel about this God and this surrender?

Let us pray: Our God with so many names, so many faces, we do believe that you love us as we are. Please help our unbelief and keep us one with Jesus and the Holy Spirit, now and forever.

All:
Amen.

REVIEW OF CONTENTS

1. Paul's enthusiasm for his life in Christ is evident in all his letters, as are his dedication to his ministry and his personal concern for those to whom he preached the gospel. When he received news that his converts were keeping the faith, Paul was quick to praise and to encourage them. When he received reports that were less favorable, Paul was equally quick in his efforts to right the situation. Paul's feelings of irritation and disappointment are particularly obvious in his letter to the churches of Galatia.

Using Paul's letter (Gal 3–4) and your companion text, *Pillars of Paul's Gospel: Galatians and Romans*, determine the reason for Paul's annoyance with the Galatians.

2. To what did Paul refer when he used the term "law"? (See companion text, pp. 63–65.)

3. In his gospel, Paul proclaimed that we are saved or justified by faith in Jesus Christ and not through the works of the law (Gal 2:15–21). In Galatians 3–4 Paul made his case for the priority of faith over the law by appealing to a series of proofs or witnesses drawn from the Galatians' own experience, from history, and from Scripture.

a. Read Galatians 3:1–5 and 4:1–20. From the Galatians' own experience, what evidence did Paul cite in support of his argument for the priority of faith?

b. Read Galatians 3:6–18. How did the experience of Abraham support Paul's argument for the priority of faith?

4. In his allegory about Abraham's sons (Gal 4:21–31), Paul invited the Galatians to discover the story of their own spiritual journey toward Christ.

a. What did Hagar and Ishmael symbolize in the religious experience of the Galatians?

b. What did Sarah and Isaac symbolize in the religious experience of the Galatians?

5. According to Paul, what purpose had the law served in God's plan of salvation?

VIDEO

The Argument of the Letter to the Galatians

As you view the video, please make note of the following:

1. What was the reasoning behind the New Testament process of writing in another's name?

_____

_____

2. How does Paul use the Scriptures in his argument against the Judaizers?

_____

_____

3. What does Christ's death to the law mean?

_____

_____

BREAK
(10 minutes)

LEARNING ACTIVITY

Prior to Jesus' saving death, membership in the people of God had been defined in terms of nationality, legal observance, and heritage. All law-abiding, circumcised descendants of Abraham were considered heirs of God's promises and blessings. But the cross of Jesus exploded the barriers that separated people as it redefined the requisites for belonging to the people of God.

1. How does Paul explain the fact that Jesus' saving death on the cross redefined eligibility for God's promises and blessings?

2. How do believers manifest their union with Jesus and the saving power of his death?

3. What is the relationship to God that has been made possible by the cross of Jesus?

4. What are the privileges and freedoms enjoyed by the new people of God, justified by the cross of Jesus Christ?

FAITH SHARING

In his stirring letter, Paul reminded the Galatians, and he reminds us also, that the saving death of Jesus has made it possible for believers to call upon God as "Abba, Father!" A surprisingly intimate form of address, Abba is the equivalent of our "Papa" or "Daddy." Because of Jesus' death, the quality of our relationship with God has been raised from mere legal observance to that of a loving, faithful relationship.

1. What are some of the names or titles by which you ordinarily call upon God?

2. What do these titles or names reveal about your relationship with God?

3. Are you comfortable in calling God "Abba" or "Daddy" or "Papa"?

4. If each of us calls upon God as "Abba, Father," what does that imply about our relationship to one another? What elements, then, should characterize our relationship to one another? How can these characteristics be better developed?

CLOSING PRAYER

A Call to Remember

Reading

Reader:
Recall these words from Paul's letter to the Galatians:
"...the law was our disciplinarian for Christ, that we might
be justified by faith" (Gal 3:24). Paul tells us that the law
was valid only until Christ came.

A Call to Respond

All:
Our compassionate and faithful God, thank you for help-
ing us grow up into new freedom, the freedom your Son
and our brother Jesus won for us through the cross. Thank
you for conquering sin and fear and law and death by rais-
ing him from the dead. We ask you to raise up in us now
new understandings of you and to heal any distorted
images of you from our childhood so that we may proclaim to all we meet the good news: our God is good and
forgiving, abounding in kindness. God, you are our faithful
Daddy, Abba; you are our tender Mommy, Em, and so we
pray:

Our Father and Mother, who art in heaven...
For the kingdom, etc.

Concluding Song

"If God Is For Us" by John Foley, S.J.

FOLLOW-UP

A. Journaling

Although he had been orthodox in his observance of Jewish law and tradition and strict in his avoidance of those who were regarded as outside the pale of salvation, Paul's encounter with the risen Jesus transformed his thinking about himself, about God, and about others. Paul expressed his faith in the universal saving power of Jesus' death in this way: "There is neither Jew nor Greek, there is neither slave nor free person, there is not male and female; for you all are one in Christ Jesus" (Gal 3:28).

How would Paul express his insights today, using twentieth-century terms and examples?

B. Additional Resources

1. Read *The Catholic Study Bible*, "Galatians," RG 507–508.

2. Read Joseph Plevnik, S.J., *What Are They Saying About Paul?*, Chapter 4, pp. 55–76.

4. Free To Be and To Do for Others

Preparation

- Read Galatians 5–6.
- Read *Pillars of Paul's Gospel: Galatians and Romans,* Chapter 8.
- Reflect on the FOCUS statement and REVIEW OF CONTENTS questions.

FOCUS

An excellent teacher and an effective preacher, Paul never left a lesson incomplete. Having established the priority of faith over the law and of the cross over circumcision, Paul then proceeded to make his message come alive with vivid illustrations and practical applications.

Keenly aware that life in Christ is an ongoing and creative process of growth, Paul wished to help the Galatians fully realize the dignity of their noble calling. By virtue of the cross of Christ, they were no longer bound by the flesh; they were free for life in the Spirit. From his own faith experience, Paul understood firsthand the tension inherent in Christian living. Each day the believer is challenged to renew the struggle of making professed faith a lived reality.

In this session, we shall explore Paul's understanding of the life of the believer who has been freed from the law and reoriented to God by the cross of Christ. We shall learn from Paul the moral imperatives that spring from the gifts of grace and freedom. With the Gala-

---

tians we shall realize that freedom from sin means freedom to be and to do for others. Finally, we shall be called upon to recognize the fact that our faith binds us not only to God but to one another in a community of mutual sharing, support, and service.

OPENING PRAYER

Opening Song

"One Bread, One Body" by John Foley, S.J. (verse 3)

Leader:
Good news! Barriers are broken and we are one. Let's sing it from verse 1 of "One Bread, One Body"!

All sing:
"Gentile or Jew, servant or free, woman or man, no more . . ." (*Refrain*)

Psalm

Leader:
Barriers are broken and we are one. Let's pray it from an adaptation of Psalm 133.

All pray:
How good it is and how pleasant when God's people live as one. This unity among us is like a dew upon the mountains, gently nourishing us.

On us God has pronounced a blessing: life forever!

Leader:
Good news! Barriers are broken and we are one.

All:
Amen. Amen.

REVIEW OF CONTENTS

1. Paul pointedly contrasts law and slavery with faith and freedom in Chapter 5 of Galatians. How does the concept of love fit in with his presentation?

2. Paul speaks directly to the Galatians in verses 7–12 of Chapter 5. How does he try to persuade the Galatians to keep on the course of the gospel he's preached to them?

3. In a recent recruiting effort, the U.S. Army challenged potential recruits to "Be all that you can be!" In a sense, Paul was issuing a similar challenge to the Galatians. Freed from the law and from the flesh by their faith in the cross of Christ, the Galatians were freed for life in the Spirit; they were free to be all that they could be, in Christ, and for one another.

a. What is the source of the freedom with which the Galatians have been gifted?

b. What did Paul mean by the cross of Christ?

c. Why did Paul call the cross a "stumbling block"?

d. Give some examples of the ways the Galatians were called to exercise their freedom and to express their faith.

4. Paul acknowledged that those who are freed by their faith in the cross of Christ are challenged to live no longer in the flesh but in the Spirit.

a. Read Galatians 5:16–21 wherein Paul lists the works of the flesh. With this list to help you, explain what Paul means by flesh.

b. Read Galatians 5:22–26. What does Paul mean by life in the Spirit?

VIDEO

The Conclusion of the Letter to the Galatians

As you view the video, please make note of the following:

1. What does "flesh" mean for Paul?

_____

_____

2. What does "Spirit" mean for Paul?

_____

_____

3. Why is the use of allegory so important in Paul's dealings with the Judaizers? Cite an allegory used by Paul and its significance.

_____

_____

BREAK
(10 minutes)

LEARNING ACTIVITY

1. In his letter to the churches in Galatia, Paul reminds us that we have been set free by Christ to serve one another in love (Gal 5:1, 13).

Choose one of the following situations and compose an appropriate definition of freedom for the individual described in that situation.

a. Helga is a homeless, unemployed mother of four. She and her children live on the streets in a large northeastern city. Winter has come early this year and the weather forecaster says it will snow soon.

b. Antonio is an elderly gentleman whose failing health has recently confined him to a wheelchair. Because his apartment building has no elevator or ramps, Antonio is unable to come and go as he needs and/or pleases.

c. Yung So lives in a country controlled by a military dictatorship. The seminary where she has been studying has been closed by the government. Yung So had to abandon her plans to become a catechist and has been conscripted for work in a factory which produces nuclear armaments.

d. Sean and Michael are brothers who were business partners. After a bitter argument, they dissolved their partnership. Still nursing grudges, they do not communicate and each refuses to attend family gatherings if the other is present.

e. Ivan is a forty-five-year-old construction worker whose inability to read has kept him from being promoted. Because his handicap makes him feel inept and uninformed, he avoids social situations as much as possible.

2. In Galatians 5–6, Paul provides a series of moral imperatives or responsibilities through which believers express their faith and freedom in Christ. Consult Galatians 5–6 and the list compiled in your companion text (p. 76).

How do these moral imperatives apply to each of the situations described in question 1?

3. Formerly circumcision had been the sign of Paul's commitment. Now he claims the cross as the sign of his faith and freedom in Christ.

Read Galatians 6:14–17.

What does Paul mean by "a new creation"?

FAITH SHARING

If Paul had spoken French, he might have entitled the last two chapters of Galatians, *"Noblesse Oblige."* Freely graced by God and gifted with the Spirit, the Galatians were challenged to live a life in proportion to their blessings. Like the believers in Galatia, we are called to exercise our freedom in service and to express our faith in love, not *in order to* be justified, but *because* we have been justified through our faith in the cross of Jesus Christ.

Paul knew well the struggle of remaining authentically free and faithful. Freedom is a gift more demanding than any law and the process of making professed faith a lived reality requires a daily renewed effort.

1. In your own life, do you experience the struggle of translating the faith you profess with your lips and mind into a reality which you live with your heart and hands and will?

2. What helps you in your daily struggle of making your professed faith a lived reality?

3. Freedom is a powerful and dynamic concept with a rich variety of meanings. What does freedom mean to you? Share whether your definition of freedom is similar to or different from others' definitions.

4. Do you agree that freedom is a gift more demanding than any law? Share your responses.

CLOSING PRAYER

Opening Song

"One Bread, One Body" (verse 2)

Fruits of the Spirit

All pray:
Thank you, Holy Spirit!

Leader:
Jesus, the gospel tells us, would often rejoice in the Holy Spirit. No wonder—for are not these fruits evident in his life: love, joy, peace, patient endurance, kindness, generosity, faith, gentleness, and self-control? Sharing his mind, his heart, and his fruitful life, let us join him in prayer.

All:
Our Father and Mother, who art in heaven . . .
For the kingdom, etc.

Leader:
In our Concluding Song, let's change the words "Many the *works*" of verse 2 to "Many the *fruits*" and sing in thanksgiving.

Concluding Song

"One Bread, One Body" (verse 2 and *Refrain*)

FOLLOW-UP

A. Journaling

In teaching the Galatians how to exercise and express their gifts of faith and freedom, Paul encouraged them to correct one another gently and to bear one another's burdens.

Read Galatians 6:1–5 and reflect upon those times in your life when you have been called to correct another and/or to bear the burdens of that person. Reflect also on those times when another has served you in this way.

Are these exercises and expressions of your faith and freedom difficult for you? Do you think they were difficult for Paul?

Compose a short prayer about the daily struggle of living free and faithful in the Spirit.

B. Additional Resources

1. Read *The Catholic Study Bible*, "Galatians," RG 508–509.

2. Read Joseph Plevnik, S.J., *What Are They Saying About Paul?*, Chapter 5, pp. 77–90.

5. All Roads Lead to Rome

Preparation

- Read Romans 1:1–3:20.
- Read *Pillars of Paul's Gospel: Galatians and Romans*, Chapters 9 and 10.
- Reflect on the FOCUS statement and REVIEW OF CONTENTS questions.

FOCUS

If Paul had ever been required to write a résumé, it probably would have resembled his letter to the believers in Rome. In this, the longest of all his surviving correspondence, Paul presented his credentials to a church he had not founded but wished to visit soon. He set forth his short-term objectives and long-range goals; after traveling to Jerusalem with a collection for the poor, Paul intended to make his way to Rome where he wished to establish a base of operations from which to launch a mission to Spain.

Detailing his plans and vision for the Roman church, Paul also shared with them his gospel. The good news is power! The good news is salvation! The good news is the very righteousness of God revealed in Jesus Christ! The good news challenges both Gentile and Jew to appropriate the gifts of God in faith!

A seasoned missionary, Paul also imparted to the Romans his understanding of humanity, universally sinful and in need of God. He shared his view of salvation history as a divine and loving plan that began with Adam and reaches unto the glory yet to be revealed, embracing without partiality every sinner in the process.

Reprising his argument for justification by faith, Paul abandoned the polemical tone of Galatians for a more studied and systematic unfolding of his thought. Although Paul was never able to realize all the plans he shared with the Roman believers, the letter he wrote to them continues to celebrate his gospel and to challenge all who read it.

OPENING PRAYER

Opening Song

To the tune of "Peace Is Flowing Like a River," by Rev. Carey Landry, sing: "God's Word is flowing like a river, flowing out from you and me . . . "

Reading (Is 55:10–11, adapted)

Leader:
Let us respond in the words of Paul.

All:
There is no holding back the Word of the Lord.

Praising God's Word

Leader:
Let us praise God's Word, using an adaptation of selected verses from Psalm 119.

Right side:
Open my eyes, O God, that I may see the wonders of your Word. I am a wayfarer on this earth. Do not hide your Word from me.

Left side:
Teach me, O Lord, the way of your Word. Give me discernment that I may pay attention to your Word and keep it with all my heart.

Right side:
I hope in your Word, in all your faithful promises. In your kindness give me life, that I may keep your Word faithfully.

Left side:
The revelation of your Word sheds light, giving understanding to the simple. I long with open heart in my yearning for your Word.

All:
Glory to God and God's holy Word. Glory to the Word made flesh. Glory to the Spirit who carries the Word to every heart. Amen.

Leader:
Thank you, our grace-full God, for the power of your Word. Thank you, Jesus for offering your life, rather than take back one iota of God's Word of good news. Thank you, Holy Spirit, for empowering us to be faithful to this good news of God's Word, and for empowering both Paul and us to spread this good Word to all we meet.

All:
Glory to God and God's holy Word. Glory to the Word made flesh. Glory to the Spirit who carries the Word to every heart. Amen. Amen.

REVIEW OF CONTENTS

1. First-century A.D. Rome enjoyed many riches, including the diversity of its people. Among the city's population of one million, there were about 40,000 to 50,000 Jews, a substantial number of whom had come to believe in Jesus as Messiah. Returning to Rome in 54 A.D.—after suffering expulsion, along with the Jews, at the hands of Claudius over the "Chrestos" (Christ) controversy—Jewish Christians found a community that had become predominantly Gentile, and conflict ensued. Paul's letter to Rome summoned the pluralistic Roman church to find its unity in Christ.

a. Using your companion text (p. 85) to guide you, identify the groups that co-existed within Rome.

b. With the aid of your companion text (pp. 87–88) and the opening address of Romans (Rom 1:1–15), list the reasons which motivated Paul to write to the Roman church.

2. From what you have learned of the composition of the Roman church, why did Paul think it necessary to make a systematic presentation of the gospel he had been preaching?

3. What "credentials" did Paul offer in order to recommend himself to the Christians in Rome? (See Romans 1:1–7.)

4. In proclaiming the gospel to the diverse ethnic elements within the Roman community, Paul employed Jewish and Greek methods of presentation.

For those familiar with the Jewish Scriptures and tradition, Paul utilized a rabbinical technique called "stringing pearls." Evident in both Galatians and Romans, this method enabled a teacher to make a point by illustrating it with a chain of Scriptural quotations.

a. Using the *NAB* footnotes to help you, locate as many Old Testament references as you can in this first section of Paul's letter to the Romans (Rom 1:1–3:20).

b. What appeal would this technique of "stringing pearls" have had for the Jewish Christian community in Rome?

5. Paul's letter to the Romans also demonstrates a technique of argumentation which originated with the Greek philosopher Dion of Borysthenes in the third century B.C. This technique, called the diatribe, enabled the author or speaker to make a point by creating an artificial conversation with an imaginary opponent. In the course of this lively conversation, questions are asked and answered, objections are rebutted, and issues are debated. For a good illustration of Paul's use of the diatribe, read Romans 2:1–11, 17–29 and Romans 3:1–9.

a. Who is Paul's imaginary opponent?

b. Considering the nature of his relationship with the Roman church, why was the diatribe an especially effective technique for Paul to use?

VIDEO

The Background of the Letter to the Romans

As you view the video, please make note of the following:

1. How does Paul's letter to the Romans differ from his other letters?

_____

_____

2. What elements characterize the doctrinal portion of the letter to the Romans?

_____

_____

3. In what two ways do scholars explain the purpose behind Paul's writing of the letter to the Romans?

_____

_____

BREAK
(10 minutes)

LEARNING ACTIVITY

1. Paul proclaimed to the Romans a gospel which fully and definitively revealed the *righteousness* of God. The Greek word which we translate as *righteousness* is the same root word from which we derive the terms *justify* and *justification*. Thus it follows that the theme of justification explored in Galatians is further developed by Paul in Romans in the dynamic concept of righteousness. When spoken of in terms of justice, the righteousness of God refers to God's gracious acquittal of undeserving sinners; and, in relational terms, righteousness refers to the mutual keeping of faith in a relationship. Throughout the history of salvation, people broke their covenants (relationships) with God; yet God remained faithful, repeatedly acquitting or forgiving them and restoring relationships with them. This saving and abiding faithfulness of God in relationships, despite human infidelity, is what Paul called the righteousness of God.

In the story of Abraham, the righteousness of God is vividly illustrated.

Read Genesis 15:1–18.

a. How was God revealed to Abram?

b. How was Abram to experience the care and faithfulness of a relationship with God?

c. In the ancient Near Eastern world, covenants or relationships were solemnly sealed, either with shared meals and/or with sacrifices. The parties entering into a relationship with one another walked between the split carcasses of the sacrificed animals, thereby agreeing to accept a similar fate if they were unfaithful to the covenant.

How was the covenant between God and Abram sealed?

d. What was Abram's response to God's righteousness?

e. In the New Testament, Jesus is presented as the incarnation of the very righteousness of God who has come among us to restore the covenant and to bring us back to a right relationship with God. Can you recall any texts which refer to the covenant with God restored by Jesus?

f. What is the appropriate response to the righteousness of God revealed in the gospel?

2. In both Hebrew and Greek, there are several words for sin, the meanings of which are: "failure to hit the mark," "a twisted, distorted condition," "rebellion," and "infidelity." Paul believed that without God's righteousness, all of humanity would remain burdened by sin.

a. How did the Gentiles miss the mark or manifest their tendency to sin? (See Romans 1:18–32.)

b. How did the Jews miss the mark? (See Romans 2:1–3:20.)

c. How are both Jews and Gentiles saved from the power of sin?

FAITH SHARING

In Paul's day, sin was described as "missing the mark." Sinners "missed the mark" by centering on themselves, rather than on God. Pre-Vatican II catechisms defined sin both as "a turning away from God" and as "a transgression against the laws of God and/or the Church." Contemporary moral theologians speak of sin as an act which contradicts one's fundamental option for God.

1. Which definition best describes your personal experience of sin? Share why this is so.

2. Because we humans are social beings, created for life within a community of persons, sin has a social dimension and its effects are contagious.

Share some examples of the social effects of sin that you have observed or experienced.

3. In his book *Whatever Became of Sin?*, the famed psychiatrist Karl Menninger suggested that modern society has lost a sense of sin because what was formerly defined as sin is now classified as "crime," "psychological dysfunction," "political or economic exploitation," "anti-social behavior," etc.

How can contemporary believers like us maintain a balanced and authentic awareness of sin?

CLOSING PRAYER

Opening Song

"If God Is For Us" by John Foley, S.J.

Invitation to Prayer

All:
A clean heart create in us, O God, and renew a faithful spirit within us. Do not cast us out from your presence and do not take your Holy Spirit from us. Give us back the joy of your salvation, and a willing spirit sustain in us. We ask you this in Jesus' name. Amen.

Rite of Cleansing

Reading (Rom 1:1–4, adapted)

Psalm (Ps 85:10–14, adapted)

Right side:
God's salvation is near indeed, glory dwelling in our land.

Left side:
Kindness and truth shall meet. Justice and peace shall kiss.

Right side:
Truth will spring from the earth and righteousness shall look down from heaven.

Left side:
Truth is named Jesus, and righteousness is our God.

Right side:
God will give benefits and our land, our hearts will yield
an increase.

Left side:
Justice shall walk before God and salvation shall be God's
way on earth.

Leader:
Let us pray with truth, justice, and peace whose name is
Jesus.

All:
Our Father and Mother, who art in heaven . . .
For the kingdom, etc.

Concluding Song

An Easter alleluia, perhaps to the tune of "Peace Is Flowing
Like a River."

FOLLOW-UP

A. Journaling

When Paul wrote to the church in Rome, he called the gospel "the power of God for the salvation of everyone who believes" (Rom 1:16). The power of the good news changed Paul in a radical way. He implored all those he met to open themselves to the transforming power of the gospel in their own lives.

Reflect upon the good news of Jesus' saving death and resurrection. How has your life been transformed by this powerful reality? What effect has the power of the gospel had upon the world? How could the power of the gospel become more effective both for you personally and on a worldwide basis?

B. Additional Resources

1. Read *The Catholic Study Bible*, "Romans," RG 472–478, and the introduction to Romans, pp. 228–230 of the New Testament.

2. Read Anthony J. Tambasco, *In the Days of Paul*, "Roman Christianity," pp. 101–112.

3. Read John Paul Heil, *Paul's Letter to the Romans*, Chapters I and II, pp. 1–39.

6. But Now...Who Can Separate Us from the Love of God?

Preparation

- Read Romans 3:21–8:39.
- Read *Pillars of Paul's Gospel: Galatians and Romans*, Chapters 11 and 15.
- Reflect on the FOCUS statement and REVIEW OF CONTENTS questions.

FOCUS

Paul was virtually unflappable in his conviction that goodness will never be overcome by evil. Having detailed the wanton state of humankind apart from God and having established the fundamental inadequacy of the law and of circumcision to effect redemption, Paul then proceeded to redirect the attention of his readers. With two small words, "But now" (Rom 3:21), Paul drew the curtain on his negative portrayal of life without the gospel in order to engage his readers in a positive discussion of the gifts and graces of life in Christ.

In studying his letter to the Galatian believers, we have already become familiar with the burden of Paul's gospel, i.e., that God has justified all of sinful humanity to himself through the cross of Jesus Christ and that faith is the only appropriate human response to God's saving gifts.

With that knowledge as our springboard we shall, during this session, soar to the heights with Paul as he celebrates the effects of justification, the freedoms of the Christian life, and the solidarity with Christ enjoyed by all in whom the Spirit dwells.

In Paul's portrayal of Abraham, we shall discover a source of union as both Jews and Greeks are called to find in him their common ancestry. In Paul's comparison of Adam and Christ, we shall learn that the ravages of sin, however severe, are no match for the power of God.

Finally we shall learn that the divine motivation for every saving act on behalf of humankind is love. As Paul regales the Romans with the indomitable love of God for the people of God, we cannot help but find courage, assurance, and strength in his words.

OPENING PRAYER

Opening Song

"Peace Is Flowing Like a River" by Rev. Carey Landry

Thanksgiving

Reader:
The love of God has been poured out into our hearts through the Holy Spirit that has been given to us (Rom 5:5).

All respond:
Thanks be to God whose love fills our hearts.

Reader:
We who are baptized into Christ Jesus are baptized into his death, buried with him through baptism into death, so that,

just as Christ was raised from the dead by the glory of the Father, we too might live in newness of life. For if we have grown into union with him through a death like his, we shall also be united with him in the resurrection (Rom 6:3–5).

All respond:
Thanks be to Christ Jesus who lives within us.

Remembering Our Baptism

All:
We who are baptized into Christ Jesus are plunged into his death, that we too might live in the newness of his life. We believe, Lord Jesus; help any unbelief and strengthen our union with you. Amen.

REVIEW OF CONTENTS

1. Paul begins this, the heart of his letter to the Romans, with the short phrase, "But now..." (Rom 3:21). Signifying a new and a positive beginning, "But now..." is Paul's way of explaining that a new era of salvation history has been initiated by the cross of Jesus Christ. It is an era of universal justification for sinners, initiated by God and appropriated by faith; it is an era wherein the righteousness of God is revealed not through the law but through the gospel.

Read Romans 5:1–11.

a. What are the effects of justification which believers experience in the new era of salvation?

b. How can Paul speak of boasting of afflictions?

c. What is the proof of God's love for us?

2. Paul extends his discussion of the effects of justification in Romans 6:1–8:17 by describing the liberation enjoyed by believers; because of the righteousness of God, believers are freed from sin, freed from death, and freed from the law. Some in the early Church misconstrued their freedoms as an excuse for license and/or libertinism (moral laxity). Romans 6:1–22 is an example of Paul's argument or diatribe against such an abuse.

a. How does Paul correct the libertines?

b. How does Christian baptism empower the believer with freedom from sin and death?

3. When Paul compared his former life to his life in Christ, he concluded that the law could not free him from sin or empower him with the strength not to sin.

Read Romans 7:7–25.

a. How does Paul express his conflict with sin?

b. To what does Paul attribute his freedom from sin?

VIDEO

Justification and the Law Yield to God's Love

As you view the video, please make note of the following:

1. What does Paul mean by the term "law"?

_____

_____

2. Why does Paul use the word redemption, i.e., "a buying back," in his address to the Roman audience?

_____

_____

3. Of what does God's righteousness consist?

_____

_____

BREAK
(10 minutes)

LEARNING ACTIVITY

1. Roman society was a pluralistic melting pot of cultures and peoples. As we've already seen, the Christian communities which emerged within that society were equally diverse. That Paul was aware of the distinctive elements and inevitable conflicts within the Roman community is evident in his portrayal of Abraham as "the father of all of us" (Rom 4:16).

Divide your small group in half, with one group representing Roman Christians of Jewish origin and the other representing Roman Christians of Gentile origin. After each subgroup has considered the text and the first part of this question, each may share its findings with the other. You may then reunite the whole small group to consider the remaining questions in this activity.

a. In Romans 4:1–25, how does Paul's portrayal of Abraham appeal to Christians of your particular background? Cite specific references.

b. If both Jew and Gentile can call Abraham father, what does that imply about their relationship to one another? How should that fact affect the life of the community?

2. In a second appeal to the Roman Christians to acknowledge their common bond, Paul reflected upon the sinful condition of humanity. By attributing the human situation to one man, Paul invoked the ancient notion of "corporate personality" whereby all of humanity was thought to be in solidarity with Adam's sin. Centuries later, Augustine would call this "original sin." Today, we understand the corrupting influence of sin in an "environmental" rather than in a

hereditary sense; because humans are socially interdependent beings, our choices and actions affect one another and the world in which we live.

Read Romans 5:12–21.

a. How did Paul explain the effects and consequences of sin?

b. How was the sinful condition of humanity remedied?

3. Just as Paul's life was radically altered by his Damascus encounter, so is the life of every believer changed by the cross of Christ. Because of our solidarity with Christ in baptism, we experience a new law, a new principle of vitality and a new direction in life. Paul called this new principle of existence the Spirit.

a. In Romans 8:1–27, how does Paul describe the solidarity of the believer with Christ?

b. Paul was acutely aware of the tension that believers experience in the day-to-day challenge of living according to the Spirit; he spoke of that tension in terms of "war" (7:23), "hostility" (8:7), and "groaning" (8:22–23). What is the reason for this tension?

c. How is the presence of the Spirit manifested in the life of the believer?

FAITH SHARING

The Roman church was a community fraught with conflict from within and from outside. Besides the daily personal challenge of life in Christ, tension simmered among Christians of diverse ethnic backgrounds. As Christianity grew more distinct from Judaism, Christians were increasingly susceptible to persecution by the Roman government (Judaism was tolerated by Rome, but Christianity was regarded as illicit).

Paul's celebration of the creative and redemptive love of God encouraged the Roman church to find its identity, its strength, and its source of union in that love.

Read Romans 8:28–39.

1. How is God shown to be a God-for-us?

2. What factors or obstacles exist in modern society that may threaten to separate people from the love of God?

3. How do you experience the love of God in your own life?

CLOSING PRAYER

Opening Song

"If God Is For Us" by John Foley, S.J.

Images of the Spirit

Litany of Thanksgiving

Leader:
Let us respond to this good news with a litany of thanksgiving, based on Romans, Chapters 5 and 8.

Reader 2:
Holy Spirit, God's own love poured out in our hearts . . .

All:
Thank you!

Reader 1:
Holy Spirit, justifying us through faith . . .

All:
Thank you!

Reader 2:
Holy Spirit, saving us, reconciling us through Jesus . . .

All:
Thank you!

Reader 1:
Holy Spirit, causing grace to overflow where sin was once in control . . .

All:
Thank you!

Reader 2:
Holy Spirit, setting us free from all condemnation and from
the law . . .

All:
Thank you!

Reader 1:
Holy Spirit, dwelling within our flesh, brimming with
life . . .

All:
Thank you!

Reader 2:
Holy Spirit, leading us from fear to friendship with God . . .

All:
Thank you!

Reader 1:
Holy Spirit, promising us a share in Christ's splendor as we
now share Christ's suffering . . .

All:
Thank you!

Reader 2:
Holy Spirit, putting our pain in perspective . . .

All:
Thank you!

Reader 1:
Holy Spirit, waiting within us, longing for God to set our
whole body free . . .

All:
Thank you!

Reader 2:
Holy Spirit, making all things work together for our good . . .

All:
Thank you!

Reader 1:
Holy Spirit, transforming us gradually into the likeness of Jesus . . .

All:
Thank you!

Leader:
Jesus is always rejoicing in the Holy Spirit. Let us join him and pray.

All:
Our Father and Mother, who art in heaven . . .
For the kingdom, etc.

Concluding Song

"The Spirit Is A-Movin'" by Rev. Carey Landry

REMINDER FOR NEXT TIME:
For the next session each participant should bring a map, atlas, or globe which will be used during the Closing Prayer.

FOLLOW-UP

A. Journaling

From his letters and from the information we can derive about him from the Acts of the Apostles, Paul gives the impression of being a dynamic, intelligent, and forceful person. Nevertheless, he was quick to admit his weakness, his personal struggle with sin, and his necessary reliance on the power of God. For all his eloquence, Paul even admitted that he was sometimes incapable of praying as he should.

Read Romans 8:26–27.

Reflect upon those times when you have struggled in expressing yourself to God. Do Paul's words give you hope? Does prayer necessarily have to be expressed in words? What are some nonverbal expressions of prayer?

B. Additional Resources

1. Read *The Catholic Study Bible*, "Romans," RG 478–481.

2. Read John Paul Heil, *Paul's Letter to the Romans*, Chapters IV and V, pp. 40–98.

7. All Who Call On the Lord Will Be Saved!

Preparation

- Read Romans 9–11.
- Read *Pillars of Paul's Gospel: Galatians and Romans*, Chapter 12.
- Reflect on the FOCUS statement and REVIEW OF CONTENTS questions.

FOCUS

Paul was an idealist; he celebrated with unabashed hope the universal saving power of God made manifest in the gospel. He gloried in the blessings of life in Christ and he even found reason to boast of his afflictions. But Paul was also a realist. He could not ignore the fact that although the righteousness of God had become incarnate among them in the person of their Messiah, the Jews, for the most part, had rejected Jesus.

Having just proclaimed that nothing can separate us from the love of God in Christ Jesus (Rom 8:39), Paul was obliged to admit that, in reality, separation did indeed exist. In Romans 9–11 and in the style of the diatribe, Paul struggles with the historical situation of Israel and the seeming contradiction to the gospel therein implied. In evidence is Paul's anguish at the plight of his former co-religionists as well as his pride in his Jewish heritage.

Paul saw the Church not as a new religion, completely distant from Judaism; rather, Paul understood the

---

Christian faith as a vital and authentic flower, sprung from the rich traditions of its Jewish roots. As Paul examines the perplexing circumstance of Jewish unbelief in Christ from the perspective of biblical history, we shall be able to trace our own faith roots. As he challenges the Jews and Gentiles in Rome to abandon haughtiness in favor of mutual awe and respect, we shall find cause to examine those prejudices which foster separateness rather than union among ourselves. As Paul looks ahead to a time when Jew and Gentile enjoy together the saving gift of God, we shall find cause to hope in a harmonious future.

OPENING PRAYER

Opening Song

"Litany" by Rev. Carey Landry

Reading (Rom 9:4–5a, 6a, 16, 32, adapted)

All:
Thanks be to God.

Psalm (Ps 80, adapted)

Right side:
O shepherd of Israel, listen! Rouse your power and come to save us. O Lord, restore us. Let your face shine upon us and we shall be saved.

Left side:
Our God, you have fed your people with the bread of tears, tears to drink in ample measure. You have left us and our enemies mock us. O Lord, restore us. Let your face shine upon us and we shall be saved.

Right side:
You brought a vine up from Egypt and transplanted it. You cleared the ground for it. It took root and filled the land. It put forth its leaves to the Sea, its shoots as far as the River.

Left side:
Why then have you broken your vine so that every passer-by plucks its fruit? The beasts of the forest lay it waste.

Right side:
Look down from heaven, O Lord, and see. Take care of this vine and protect what your right hand has planted. Then we will no more withdraw from you.

Left side:
Give us new life and we will call on your name. O Lord, restore us. Let your face shine upon us and we shall be saved.

Leader:
Let us pray. Keep all your people—Israel, your Christian community, all the nations—in your heart, our God. Forgive us our divisions of race and culture, our sexism and nationalism, our lording it over the little ones of this earth. Keep us one—neither Gentile nor Jew, neither slave nor free, neither rich nor poor, neither male nor female—but one in Christ, your Vine, our source of life. We ask that we may be rooted and grounded in him with all our brothers and sisters around the world, through the power of your Holy Spirit who lives with you and in us, one God, forever.

All:
Amen.

REVIEW OF CONTENTS

1. Paul's conversion to Christ was genuine and absolute; he held back nothing as he spent himself in the service of the good news. But Paul was not oblivious to his Jewish roots or to the fact that God had chosen Judaism as the forum within which to speak the saving Word. Because of this, Paul was especially saddened by the reality that the majority of his fellow Jews did not accept Jesus as their Messiah. Paul believed that the Jews had been blessed by God with certain privileges which should have prepared them for recognizing and accepting Jesus.

What were these privileges and/or blessings? (See Romans 9:4–5; 10:14–21.)

2. How did Paul express his personal anguish with regard to the Jewish rejection of the good news?

3. Why was the fact that the Jews did not recognize Jesus a difficulty for the early Church?

4. With what images or metaphors did Paul illustrate the sovereign power of God? (See Romans 9:14–24.)

5. With what images or metaphors did Paul illustrate the union of the Jews and Gentiles in Christ? (See Romans 11:16–24.)

VIDEO

The Love of God in the Letter to the Romans

As you view the video, please make note of the following:

1. How does Paul explain what we have come to term "original sin"?

_____

_____

2. Why did Paul specifically address the Gentile members of the Roman community concerning freedom from the slavery of sin and selfish desire?

_____

_____

3. What purpose does the imagery of baptism play in the letter to the Romans?

_____

_____

BREAK
(10 minutes)

LEARNING ACTIVITY

1. Throughout the course of biblical history, it seems that God chose people who by human standards were "least likely to succeed" in order to manifest the plan of salvation. In his letter to the Romans, Paul cites examples of the divine penchant for surprising choices.

a. Locate and list as many of these examples as you can in Romans 9–11.

b. What explanation does Paul offer with regard to God's surprising choices?

c. Can you think of any other surprising examples of divine election in biblical history (Old Testament or New Testament)?

d. Given the nature of God's elective plan and gratuitous saving mercy, what response to God and to the gifts of God does Paul advise?

e. How is that response to be manifested?

2. Paul had profound faith in God's providence and in the universal scope of salvation. Even though it seemed that Israel's lack of faith had resulted in its exclusion from that plan, Paul nevertheless believed and asserted that God in righteousness would provide for Israel's salvation.

a. How does Paul express his faith in the universal scope of salvation?

b. What facts in biblical history illustrate God's righteousness and faithfulness on Israel's behalf?

c. As anguished as he was at Israel's separation from Christ, Paul understood that in the overall scheme of salvation, God would cause all things to work together for good (cf. Rom 8:28). What "good" did Paul find in Israel's rejection of Jesus and the gospel?

FAITH SHARING

Over the past several years and due in part to the famous 1977 television miniseries "Roots," many of us have experienced an increased interest in our ancestral origins. But whereas many of us trace our familial roots to discover our ethnic distinctiveness and uniqueness, Paul invites us to trace our spiritual roots to discover our unity and our common heritage.

1a. In whom does Paul challenge both Jews and Gentiles to find their common ancestry?

b. What is the bond that unites and maintains the unity of both Jew and Gentile to their spiritual ancestors and to one another?

2. At the Second Vatican Council, the assembled participants declared, "For all peoples comprise a single community, and have a single origin, since God made the whole human race to dwell over the entire face of the earth. One also is their final goal: God" (*Declaration on the Relationship of the Church to Non-Christian Religions*, 1). In their book *Megatrends 2000, Ten Directions for the 1990s*, John Naisbitt and Patricia Aburdene suggested that the third Christian millennium will be characterized by a new era of globalization wherein the accent will be on the worldwide networking of people and resources rather than on separatism and rivalry.

Given these views of the world we live in and of the world as it will be, what do you think is the role of the believer?

3. Reflect for a few moments on your spiritual roots. By means of a simple illustration (a spiritual family tree), indicate those persons who have fostered in you the rich heritage of the faith. These persons may be living or dead, contemporaries or historical figures of the past, and of any faith.

CLOSING PRAYER

Opening Song

"Here I Am, Lord" by Dan Schutte, S.J. (verse 1)

God's Will

"Everyone" Images

Responsorial Psalm (Ps 40, selected verses, adapted)

All:
Here I am, Lord. I come to do your will.

Reader:
I waited for the Lord . . . God put a new song in my mouth. How many your wondrous works, O God! How many your plans for us and our peace!

All:
Here I am, Lord. I come to do your will.

Reader:

You do not want sacrifice or oblations, but ears open to you. I said, "Behold I come; to do your will is my delight. I announce your love in the vast assembly."

All:

Here I am, Lord. I come to do your will.

Reader:

I have spoken of your faithfulness and your salvation. I do not keep your kindness and your truth secret. You know I will never stop telling all peoples how loving you are.

All:

Here I am, Lord. I come to do your will.

Leader:

With Jesus, we pray that God's will, God's passionate desires for us, be done on earth as they are done in heaven.

All:

Our Father and Mother, who art in heaven . . .
For the kingdom, etc.

Leader:

Let us go in peace to make God's peace visible in our lives.

Concluding Song

"Here I Am, Lord" (verse 2)

FOLLOW-UP

A. Journaling

After coming to the end of his exploration into Israel's role in God's saving plan, Paul paused to marvel at the mystery of God's ways. Unable to fully explain or even to understand the unsearchable wisdom of God, Paul was nevertheless a believer. With one last word he ends the doctrinal presentation of his letter to the Romans: AMEN. Derived from Hebrew, "Amen" implies certainty, trust, and faith.

Are there times in your life when God's ways seem unsearchable and mysterious?

What enables you to accept the mystery and to respond with a faith-filled and trusting AMEN?

B. Additional Resources

1. Read *The Catholic Study Bible*, "Romans," RG 481–482.

2. Read John Paul Heil, *Paul's Letter to the Romans*, Chapter VI, pp. 99–135.

8. Put On the Lord Jesus Christ!

Preparation

- Read Romans 12:1–15:13.
- Read *Pillars of Paul's Gospel: Galatians and Romans*, Chapters 13 and 14.
- Reflect on the FOCUS statement and REVIEW OF CONTENTS questions.

FOCUS

Jewish Christians in Rome would have recognized the ethical directives with which Paul ended his letter as *Halakah*. A rabbinical term derived from the verb "to walk," *Halakah* referred to the manner of living which was in accord with the Torah. But Christ had replaced the Torah or law as the absolute norm of conduct. As Paul summoned the Roman believers to "put on the Lord Jesus Christ," he also challenged them to embrace a new norm of conduct, driven by love and inspired by their own experience of the generous mercies of God.

Gentile Christians in Rome would have understood Paul's ethical directives as *paranesis*. A Greek term, *paranesis* referred to persuasive exhortation, the purpose of which was to effect a moral response. Addressing himself to both Jew and Gentile, Paul concluded this, his most important letter, with an appeal to unity and harmony within the Roman church. Timeless in their value and relevance, Paul's words reach beyond first-century Rome and speak to all the

---

redeemed. Transformed by life in Christ, believers are called to relinquish all self-interested concerns in order to live by faith for one another and for the Lord. Graced by the gospel and gifted for service, we are called to make sacred our existence in this world as we wait in hope for the glory yet to come.

OPENING PRAYER

Opening Song

"Song of Jesus Christ" by John Sheehan, arranged by Rev. Carey Landry

Reading (Acts 9:1–5)

All:
Thanks be to God.

Psalm (Ps 72, adapted)

Right side:
O God, with your judgment endow us, and with your justice, each of us, that we may bring justice to your afflicted ones.

Left side:
Help us defend the afflicted among the people, save the children of the poor, and crush the oppressor.

Right side:

May we help the poor when they cry out, and the burdened when there is no one to help them. Let us have pity on the lowly and the poor.

Left side:

Keep us from fraud and violence, but let us pray for one another continually, and be a blessing for your people.

All:

Glory to God who calls us to be one body;
Glory to Jesus who lives deep within us;
Glory to the Spirit who is the bond among us, now and forever. Amen.

Concluding Song

"One Bread, One Body" by John Foley, S.J. (*Refrain* only)

REVIEW OF CONTENTS

"Put on the Lord Jesus Christ!" With these words, Paul acknowledged the fact that believers are called to embrace Jesus as the new norm of conduct for their lives. Those who "put on Christ" are to live according to a new value system, motivated by love, expressed in service, and concerned with a union which respects individual differences. Paul encouraged the Romans and all believers to manifest their commitment to Christ in every aspect of their lives.

1. How are believers to manifest their commitment to Christ in their personal lives? (See Romans 12:1–2.)

2. What metaphor did Paul use to describe the union of those who had put on Christ?

3. How are believers to manifest their commitment to Christ within the community? (See Romans 12:9–21.)

4. How are believers to manifest their commitment to Christ in their political and/or civic lives? (See Romans 13:1–10.)

5. What overriding action does Paul encourage among the believers in Romans 14 and 15?

VIDEO

Weak and Strong Christians: Who Are They?

As you view the video, please make note of the following:

1. How does Paul seem to speak of the world of which we are now a part?

_____

_____

2. In what way does Israel fit into God's plan?

_____

_____

3. How do Paul's teachings apply to Christian living today?

_____

_____

BREAK
(10 minutes)

LEARNING ACTIVITY

1. Paul's description of the love which should characterize believers (Rom 12:9–21) echoes the teachings of Jesus as gathered together and preserved in the Sermon on the Mount (Mt 5–7; Lk 6:20–49). Throughout the centuries, this quality of Christian living has been variously described as "an impossible ideal," "perfectionist legalism," and/or a short-term "interim ethic" rather than a long-term moral challenge.

a. Do Jesus' demands as preached by Paul represent an impossible challenge?

b. Using what you have learned of his ideas and theology, how do you think Paul would answer this question?

2. In his study on human moral maturation, educational psychologist Lawrence Kohlberg cites three stages of development. In the first stage, the individual's behavior is motivated by fear of punishment and/or hope of reward. In the next stage the person conforms his or her behavior to that of his or her peers and/or to society, with its customs and laws. In the next stage, or at the highest level of moral development, the individual commits himself or herself to a particular decision or behavior based upon personal conviction.

In his letters Paul calls believers to the highest level of moral living. What evidence can you find in Romans 12–15 to support this fact?

3. Conflict over dietary practices and the observance of certain feasts threatened the unity of the Roman church.

a. With the help of your companion text (pp. 129–130) and Romans 14:1–15:13, identify those whom Paul referred to as the weak and the strong.

b. What advice did Paul give to the differing groups within the Roman community?

c. The twentieth-century Church is also characterized by diversity. What groups can you identify within the Church today? Is Paul's first century advice about communal unity still relevant today?

FAITH SHARING

1. Jesus became flesh and lived among us as the "man for others." He called those whom he justified to live by faith "in him," and "for one another." In his letter to the Romans, Paul reminds us that we, though many, are one body in Christ and that we have gifts to share with one another (Rom 12:5–6).

a. Name and describe some of the gifts for ministry with which the Roman believers were graced (Rom 12:6–8).

b. Are these gifts still in evidence in the Church today? Name some people—local, national, or international figures—in whom these gifts (and/or other gifts) are manifested.

2. Since the Second Vatican Council, renewed attention has been focused on the unique gifts and call to ministry of the laity. Calling their service to the world, "the apostolate of the social milieu," the Council delegates underscored the fact that "there are many persons who can hear the gospel and recognize Christ only through the laity who live near them" (*Decree on the Apostolate of the Laity*, Chapter III, 13).

a. How can you be a minister of the good news for your family? Your friends? Your parish? Your neighborhood? The people with whom you work?

b. Has your study of Paul's gospel made you more aware of the unique gifts with which *you* build up the body of Christ?

CLOSING PRAYER

Opening Song

"One Bread, One Body" by John Foley, S.J. (verse 1)

A Call to Remember

Reading (Rom 12:6–8, adapted)

Hymn of Love (Rom 12:9–18, adapted)

Psalm (Ps 116, selected verses, adapted)

Right side:
How can I repay our God for all these gifts and goodness?
The cup of salvation I will take up and call on the name of
the Lord.

Left side:
A sacrifice of thanksgiving I will make. My vows to the
Lord I will pay in the presence of God's people.

Leader:
We offer ourselves as living sacrifice, our grace-full God, in
union with Jesus' great act of thanksgiving to you. Keep us
alert to your Spirit who is your love poured into our hearts,
so that we may love with your love, love AS Jesus continues to love. Keep us, who love you in all things, one. We
pray together as sisters and brothers.

All:
Our Father and Mother, who art in heaven . . .
For the kingdom, etc.

Leader:
Let us bless each other with peace, offering each other Christ's peace as we say thank you and goodbye. (All exchange a greeting of peace.)

Concluding Song

"We Thank You Father" by Gregory Norbet, O.S.B.

FOLLOW-UP

A. Journaling

When Paul finally came to Rome, it was not for the visit he had planned. He came to Rome as a prisoner and remained there under house arrest until his death. But nothing could imprison the power of the good news as he preached it. For centuries, believers have been challenged, chastened, and comforted by Paul's words.

1. What is the most important thing you have learned from Paul?

2. In what way has your study of his gospel changed your life?

B. Additional Resources

1. Read *The Catholic Study Bible*, "Romans," RG 482–484.

2. Read John Paul Heil, *Paul's Letter to the Romans*, Chapter VII, pp. 136–161.